FOR LUCAS

The author wishes to extend special thanks to:

Dr. Zahi Hawass
Director General of the Giza Pyramids and Saqqara
for his assistance during my stay in Egypt, and for his help with the text and artwork.

Dr. Ogden Goelet
Department of Near Eastern Studies
New York University
for his thoughtful reading of and suggestions for the manuscript.

Editor: Stuart Waldman
Design: Lesley Ehlers Design

Distributed in North America by Firefly Books Ltd.,
3680 Victoria Park Ave., Willowdale, Ontario, M2H3KI

Library of Congress Cataloging-in-Publication Data
Mann, Elizabeth. 1948-
The Great Pyramid / by Elizabeth Mann : with illustrations by
Laura Lo Turco.
p.   cm.
Includes index.
Summary: A history of the construction of the Great Pyramid at
Giza and the civilization that produced it.
ISBN 0-9650493-1-0
1. Great Pyramid (Egypt) — Juvenile literature. 2. Egypt–
– Civilization — To 332 B.C. —Juvenile literature. [1. Great Pyramid
(Egypt) 2. Pyramids — Egypt. 3. Egypt — Antiquities. 4. Egypt-
-Civilization —To 332 B.C.] I. Lo Turco, Laura, 1963–   ill.
II. Title.
DT61.M297   1996
932 — dc20   96-21337

Printed in Hong Kong

The Great Pyramid

A WONDERS OF THE WORLD BOOK

BY ELIZABETH MANN

WITH ILLUSTRATIONS BY LAURA LO TURCO

MIKAYA PRESS

NEW YORK

The boy bent to lift a basket. The harvest had been good and the whole village had turned out to help thresh the wheat. Oxen moved slowly, trampling the dry stalks and cracking open the hard husks. Villagers tossed the stalks in the air and the hot wind blew them away. The boy's job was to gather the wheat kernels that were left behind. As he swung the basket to his shoulder, he looked out toward the Nile and stopped in surprise.

Strangers were stepping out of a boat. Word passed quickly that they were from the pharaoh. People gathered to hear what they had to say.

The news was exciting. The pharaoh needed workers. Royal messengers had never bothered to come to such a tiny village before, but the boy had heard about them. Farmers from a larger village nearby had gone with the pharaoh's men the summer before and they had brought back many stories. They talked about how hard and dangerous the work was. They complained, but they also boasted. They seemed proud to be doing something so important.

The boy stood with the men of his village. Was he old enough to be chosen? He stood on tiptoe to look taller. One of the pharaoh's messengers beckoned to him. He raced forward and told the scribe his name.

When the harvest was over, the boy joined the other men as they began their journey. They traveled many miles by boat down the Nile. None of them had ever been so far from the village. The boat turned into a narrow canal heading toward the western desert. The canal widened into a harbor, and beyond it a plateau rose like a cliff from the valley floor. On top of the plateau, stretched across the sky, was an immense, unfinished stone structure. The boy could not believe that a building could be so huge. Thousands of workers, looking as small as insects, moved busily around the gigantic construction site. This was the important work to be done. This was the Great Pyramid of the pharaoh Khufu.

And so it might have been for a boy living in ancient Egypt.

4,500 years later we can easily imagine his feelings as he stood before the Great Pyramid. We are just as astonished by it today as he must have been then, and a lot more puzzled.

Ancient Egyptians had no iron tools. How did they quarry and shape 2,300,000 stone blocks? They had no vehicles with wheels. How were they able to move and lift blocks weighing several tons? And why was it built? What inspired a nation of primitive farmers to create a building that, for over 40 centuries, was the tallest in the world?

The story of the Great Pyramid begins hundreds of years before the reign of pharaoh Khufu. It begins with the first people to settle along the Nile River.

The Nile is a long ribbon of water that winds for hundreds of miles through a wide desert. Every year, heavy rains at the river's source high in the African mountains make it overflow. For three months, the entire valley is under water. When the land reappears, it is covered with wet, black silt. This fertile soil that the Nile leaves behind is ideal for growing crops.

Long ago, people from wandering tribes left the harsh, dry desert and began farming the rich valley soil. They scattered seeds by hand and carried buckets of water for irrigation. They dried mud bricks in the sun and built homes on high ground above the level of the flood. The crops were successful and the villages prospered.

Horus, the sky god, was the son of Osiris. He was also the falcon god.

The all-powerful sun god, Re, had many different names and identities. Here he has a falcon head, but he was also shown as a ram, a beetle, and even a human.

Hathor, goddess of joy and music and love, appeared as a cow.

Early Egyptians observed the world around them. They noticed many cycles that seemed to repeat endlessly. The sun went down every night, but it always came up the next morning. Cropland disappeared during every flood, but it always reappeared. People were reassured by the repetition of nature's cycles. If every ending was followed by a new beginning, there was balance and order in the world. Egyptians called this balance *ma'at.* With *ma'at,* life was safe. Without it, there was chaos.

Osiris was the god of the Land of the Dead. He was shown wrapped in white linen like a mummy.

Thoth was the god of writing and wisdom. In this sculpture he is a baboon, but Egyptian artists often showed him as a human with the head of a long-beaked bird.

Jackal-headed Anubis was the god of mummification.

Maintaining *ma'at* was important, and they turned to their gods for help. There were hundreds of them – strange, magical beings, who controlled every aspect of Egyptian life. Some were local village gods. Others were worshipped throughout the country. Above them all was Re, god of the sun.

Long, complicated stories were told about the gods, myths that changed constantly and often contradicted each other. The religion that grew out of these myths may seem peculiar and far-fetched to us, but Egyptians believed in it wholeheartedly. They worshipped their gods without question.

One important belief was simple and unchanging. Egyptians believed in life after death. They thought that a person's spirit, or *ka,* was reborn in the Land of the Dead, where it would live forever. Death, rebirth, and afterlife formed another cycle, as important as the rising and setting of the sun. To preserve it, they made a great effort to insure an afterlife for every *ka*.

The *ka* lived the same life in the Land of the Dead that the person had lived on earth. It used the same tools and pots, wore the same jewelry, ate the same food. Though it lived in the Land of the Dead, the *ka* had to return to the body for nourishment. To make sure that it had a place to come back to, the grave was covered with a rectangular mud brick structure called a *mastaba*. The *mastaba* protected the body and the household items that were buried with it. It was, in a way, a home for the dead person's *ka*.

The tops of mastabas were rounded. According to an early myth, the world was once an endless ocean. A mound of earth appeared in the water, and there all life began. Egyptians imitated the shape of that important first mound when they built their mastabas.
A mastaba could be large or small. One like this, for a wealthy person, might have contained 30 rooms. Offerings for the ka were placed outside .

Another important religious belief involved Egypt's rulers. People thought that a pharaoh was the god, Horus, on earth. Horus was directly descended from Re, the sun god. When a pharaoh died, his *ka* would not have an ordinary afterlife in the Land of the Dead. It would join Re, and live forever among the gods.

Egyptians imagined that the sun traveled across the sky in a boat like the ones they used on the Nile.

A living pharaoh, a god on earth, could do much to protect Egypt from chaos. He could keep the nation strong and unified, and defeat all enemies. A dead pharaoh was able to do far more wonderful things for his people. Gliding across the heavens each day with Re in the solar boat, he could even affect the most important of all the natural cycles, the rising and setting of the sun. Egyptians didn't want to lose this special protection, so they worked especially hard for the pharaoh's afterlife.

Djoser's brilliant architect, Imhotep, invented the art of building with stone. Stone is stronger than mud brick, and lasts forever, so others were quick to follow his example. Stone was used throughout the country to build tombs and temples, but never houses or palaces. The places where people lived were still made of mud brick. The ancient Egyptians' choice of building materials shows clearly that the afterlife was more important to them than earthly life.

Pharaohs' tombs were larger and more elaborate than those of ordinary people. They contained priceless jewelry, extraordinary statues, and many household objects for the *ka* to use in the afterlife. Royal *mastabas* were sometimes as large as palaces.

In 2630 B.C., a pharaoh named Djoser built an unusual tomb at Saqqara, near the capital city of Memphis. It began as a *mastaba,* but it was made of stone blocks instead of mud bricks. Its shape changed as more and more layers were added. When it was finished, it looked like a gigantic stairway. The 200-foot tall Step Pyramid was an imposing sight, visible for miles in the empty desert. Pharaohs who came after Djoser were inspired by it, and they, too, built stone pyramids instead of mud brick *mastabas.*

Less than 100 years later, in 2550 B.C., Khufu took the throne. He followed the tradition of the pharaohs who had ruled before him and became the god, Horus, on earth.

Later in his reign, however, Khufu did something that no other pharaoh had done before. He declared that, in addition to being Horus, he was also Re on earth. It was quite extraordinary, even for a king of Khufu's power, to claim such a thing. By taking on the identity of the mighty sun god, Khufu established himself as the mightiest pharaoh ever.

Khufu often traveled on the Nile, visiting temples and performing ceremonies to honor the gods. He was accompanied by priests wearing leopard skins.

Papyrus plants, like the ones resting on the man's shoulder, grew in marshy areas along the Nile. Papyrus was used for paper, but Egyptians also made ropes, baskets, and even boats from the tall stalks.

Khufu worked hard at ruling his vast kingdom. His influence reached into every household in Egypt. He appointed 42 governors, one for each district in the country. It was their job to enforce his laws and collect taxes. Throughout Egypt, his officials kept track of the crops and livestock. Scribes recorded every detail of government business in hieroglyphics on long rolls of papyrus. Keeping order in the government was part of maintaining *ma'at*.

Scribes sat cross-legged and painted on the papyrus scrolls spread across their knees. Since most Egyptians couldn't read or write, scribes were greatly respected for their skills.

Money had not been invented when Khufu ruled, so taxes were paid with cattle and grain. Here, scribes are counting cattle and writing down the taxes to be paid.

In hieroglyphics, each little picture represents a sound. In our form of writing, sounds are represented by letters.

Egypt prospered under Khufu and life was luxurious. He led extravagant sailing excursions, hunting expeditions, and fishing trips. Officials, nobles, and priests joined him at his palace for banquets. The guests wore fine linen, scented wigs, and dramatic eye makeup. Their gold jewelry was heavy with precious stones. While musicians and dancers performed tirelessly, servants carried trays heavy with meat and bread and fruit. The wine flowed freely.

The pleasures and duties of a pharaoh's earthly life would only last a few years. His *ka* was expected to exist for eternity, so a pharaoh's most important responsibility was to prepare for the afterlife. For Khufu it was especially important. He had declared himself to be the greatest pharaoh ever. Now he had to build the greatest tomb ever.

Wine makers were kept busy supplying the royal household.

One woman strums her harp while
the other sings.

Hippopotamus hunting was as thrilling as it was dangerous. The hunters stood in
small boats and threw wooden spears at the huge animals.

He chose the location carefully. It had to be on high ground, above the flood waters. Like all Egyptian graves, it had to be in the Western Desert, close to where the Land of the Dead was believed to be. To set himself apart, Khufu wanted a site where no pharaoh had been buried before.

The Giza Plateau was all of these things, and more.

The plateau is solid limestone, firm enough to support the tremendous weight of a 50-story, 13-acre pyramid. There is so much limestone that quarries on the plateau could provide most of the stone blocks needed to build the pyramid. It was a practical location, and, with cliffs soaring 100 feet up from the valley, a very impressive one.

Khufu alerted his governors that he would need laborers. Every summer thousands and thousands of farmers would come to work for him while the Nile flooded their fields.

Once the workers arrived at Giza, bread had to be provided for them. They needed shelter and clothing. They needed tools, sharpened and in good repair. And they needed to be organized so that they did not get in each other's way on the construction site. It was a phenomenal undertaking. Work gangs were assembled, each with an overseer. The workers chose names for their gangs like "Enduring Gang" and "Beloved of Khufu." They painted them proudly in red on the stone blocks.

Quarries all over Egypt echoed with the sound of mallets as massive blocks were carved out of the surrounding stone. From Fayyum came dark, greenish-black basalt for the temple floors. From Aswan came granite, so heavy that a single block weighed 40 tons. And from Tura came the fine white limestone to cover the outside of the pyramid.

Stone from quarries hundreds of miles away came by boat to a man-made harbor near the Giza Plateau.
Using only primitive tools, Egyptian stonemasons shaped blocks so skillfully that a knife couldn't slide between them.

Papyrus boats would have sunk under the weight of the stone used at Giza. Boat builders had to learn to build much larger boats out of wood.

The Great Pyramid had a tremendous effect on Egyptians who lived 4,500 years ago. Egyptians were farmers. Their lives had always centered on their fields and livestock, their villages and local gods. But those who left their homes every year and gathered at the Giza Plateau became part of a bigger world, a bigger society. They were loyal, not just to their village, but to the great work they were doing. By contributing to the afterlife of their pharaoh, they were insuring prosperity for all of Egypt. When they returned to their villages, they brought with them the sense of belonging to a larger community.

For some, the change in their lives was even greater. Many skilled workers did not return to their fields. They stayed at Giza with their families and worked year round for the pharaoh. Freed from the hard labor of farming, they developed remarkable talents as artists, boat builders, goldsmiths, and stonemasons.

Goldsmiths weighed the gold before they melted it (above). They put finishing touches on a necklace and a belt (below).

In the twenty-third year of his reign, the pharaoh Khufu died. Mourners stood along the Nile, striking sticks together and weeping as the funeral boat passed by. Priests waited at the valley temple to receive the body of their king. The painstaking job of mummification began.

After 70 days, the body was ready for burial.

Egyptians developed mummification to preserve the body so the ka could recognize it when it returned for nourishment. The organs were removed and the body was packed in a kind of salt to dry it out. The finished mummy was wrapped in linen cloth and placed in a wooden coffin.

The valley temple was connected by the causeway to another temple at the base of the pyramid. Both were used for important religious ceremonies before and after Khufu's death.

The coffin containing Khufu's mummy was lowered into the granite sarcophagus deep within the pyramid. The heavy lid was closed. Khufu's body was sealed inside the Great Pyramid. His *ka* was free.

Offerings for the ka included cattle, ducks, bread, and fruit.

Khufu left behind a large organization of priests and workers. He had chosen them as carefully as he had planned his pyramid. Though the priests were active in the religion while Khufu was alive, it wasn't until after his death that they became vitally important.

They were the guardians of Khufu's afterlife. It was their solemn responsibility to do everything possible on earth to insure the *ka's* eternal existence. They performed ceremonies honoring the gods. They protected the pyramid from tomb robbers. They made offerings of food to the *ka*.

Most importantly, they passed their knowledge of these rituals on to younger priests and workers, so that Khufu's *ka* would be nourished and protected forever.

For a time, the priests made their ritual offerings accompanied only by the sound of the wind on the deserted plateau. But before long, Giza was alive again with workers' shouts and pounding. Khafre, Khufu's son, had chosen a slope just above the Great Pyramid as the site for his own tomb. Now that he was the pharaoh, he, too, had to prepare for his afterlife.

When Khafre died, his son, Menkaure, built the third and last giant pyramid on the Giza Plateau. Pharaohs who came after him built pyramids, but they were smaller and not as well made. Egypt was changing. Pharaohs no longer had the wealth and power needed to build grand tombs.

As the pharaohs grew weaker, the people suffered great hardship. For several years in a row, the Nile did not rise high enough to bring new soil to the valley. Crops withered and died in the fields. People were starving, and they lost faith in their pharaohs. Governors and nobles fought for power. Chaos ruled the land.

Eventually the bad times passed. Stronger pharaohs regained control of the country, but it was many years before they regained the trust of their people.

Khufu's burial chamber was plundered long ago. Statues, jewelry, all traces of his wealth were stolen or destroyed. Even his mummy was taken. The only image of Khufu that exists today is a tiny, damaged statue barely three inches tall.

His vision of an eternal afterlife was shattered. But Khufu achieved a different kind of immortality.

After 45 centuries his pyramid still stands on the Giza Plateau.

The pyramid looks different today. The gold capstone has disappeared. (The metal pole on top shows how tall the pyramid used to be.) The smooth, white "facing" stone is gone, too, leaving the rough "core" limestone exposed.

The Great Pyramid has been measured, photographed, x-rayed, and studied more than any building in the world. Many theories about Khufu and his tomb exist, and they rarely agree. This book is based on the most widely respected theories and the most recent archaeological evidence, but it is by no means the whole story.

There are things we'll never know. Most traces of the daily lives of ancient Egyptians disappeared when their mud brick homes crumbled to dust. Many of the stone tombs and temples that remain have been robbed or damaged.

Archaeologists still sift the sands of the Giza Plateau, looking for clues. And they are finding them. Small pieces of pots, bone, and stone can tell remarkable stories to those who know how to read them. Just two years ago it was discovered that an area of scattered rocks beside the Great Pyramid had once been a fourth small pyramid.

More is being learned every day, but the story of Khufu and his Great Pyramid will probably never be finished. Perhaps that's why it is endlessly intriguing.

GLOSSARY

Aswan - Where granite was quarried, nearly 600 miles up the river from Giza.

Djoser - Pharaoh, builder of the the first pyramid, the Step Pyramid.

Fayyum - Where basalt was quarried.

Giza Plateau - Site of the pyramids of Khufu, Khafre, and Menkaure.

hieroglyphics - Ancient form of writing in which pictures, rather than letters, represent sounds.

Imhotep - Djoser's architect, inventor of the art of building with stone.

ka - Spirit, or soul, of a person. The *ka* lives on after the person has died.

Khafre - Pharaoh, son of Khufu, builder of the second large pyramid at Giza. Sometimes known by the Greek name, Chephren.

Khufu - Pharaoh who built the Great Pyramid. Sometimes known by the Greek name, Cheops.

ma'at - Order, harmony, and balance in the world.

mastaba - Rectangular structure built over a grave to protect the contents.

Menkaure - Pharaoh, son of Khafre, grandson of Khufu, builder of the third Giza pyramid. Sometimes known by the Greek name, Mycerinus.

Memphis - Capital city of ancient Egypt.

Saqqara - Site of Djoser's Step Pyramid. Many other pharaohs and nobles were also buried there.

Tura - Where white "facing" block limestone was quarried.

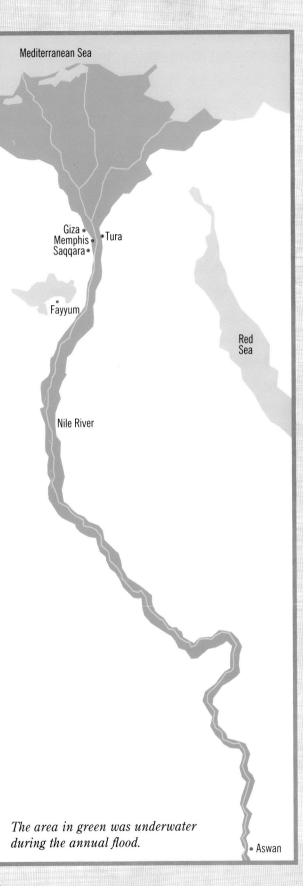

The area in green was underwater during the annual flood.

INDEX

CREDITS

Werner Forman/Art Resource, NY: *pp. 9* (center), *21* (bottom and center), *26* (top left), *29* (top right)

Kenneth Garrett: *pp. 18, 21* (top), *30, 31, 36*

Giraudon/Art Resource, NY: *pp. 8* (center), *9* (right), *19* (bottom, left and right)

David W. Hamilton/The Image Bank: *pp. 44-45*

Jürgen Liepe: *p. 43*

Erich Lessing/Art Resource, NY: *pp. 8* (left), *19* (top)

Laura Lo Turco: *pp. 5, 7, 11, 12, 13, 17, 22-23, 25, 26-29, 32, 33, 35, 39, 40*

Scala/Art Resource, NY: *p. 9* (left)

Paul Trummer/The Image Bank: *p. 14*

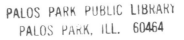

0 500 1000 1500